A History of "Peny's Hey"

A History of "Peny's Hey"

PATRICIA ANN DYSON

Published in 2016 by JP&A Dyson
Copyright Patricia Ann Dyson

ISBN 978-1-909935-17-4

All rights reserved. No part of this publication may be reproduced or transmitted in any form or by any means, or stored in any retrieval system without prior written permission. Whilst every effort is made to ensure that all information contained within this publication is accurate, no liability can be accepted for any mistakes or omissions, or for losses incurred as a result of actions taken in relation to information provided.

**Registered with the IP Rights Office
Copyright Registration Service
Ref: 3060264704**

CONTENTS

	1	Introduction	1
	2	Renovation	5
	3	Early records about Hey	15
	4	Ownership of Hey	19
	5	Tenants at Hey	21
	6	Architecture of the house	27
Appendix		Dendrochronology report	33

Chapter One
INTRODUCTION

One warm spring morning in 1983 I collected our small son, Paul, from nursery school and we walked home up the hill and over the fields. As we passed the old house almost at the top of the hill I lifted Paul up so that he could see the large pig snuffling around the grassy garden.

That autumn I went picking blackberries with the children from the nursery school. We climbed the hill on our way to the fields, and stood and looked through the gate at the hens and the tractor in the farmyard of the old house.

The next time the house touched my life was in hospital almost a year later. I was having an amniocentesis and the nurse holding my hand and diverting my attention told me more about the house. It turned out that she was married to the son of the family who owned the plant nursery next to the old house. She told me that one of the men keeping pigs in the house had suffered a heart attack in the barn and died. There was also a rumour that Kirklees Council were considering selling the property.

Then one day in October 1985 I wheeled our nine-month-old daughter to school to collect Paul. Looking up the hill I saw a large notice on the old house. The council were indeed selling it. The following Saturday we walked up to have a closer look and I went into Huddersfield to collect a tender form. Shock, horror – I discovered that the closing date for submitting tenders was the Friday of that week – and this was Wednesday! No time to take expert advice. We filled in the form, took a stab at a reasonable offer, and returned the form the day after.

In the ensuing weeks, we heard that at least one other local person had tendered: a builder wanted to put six houses on the site, and the RSPCA were interested in it for kennels. We had been looking at old properties to renovate for some time, and had in fact already tendered for a property at Hall Bower. Fortunately that bid was unsuccessful, but we didn't know this when we tendered for the house up Hey Lane. A major worry for a short time! In November we learnt that our bid had been successful, and preparations started for the mammoth task in hand.

The house was derelict. The two-storey cottage hadn't been lived in for 15 years, and the single-storey one for even longer. We later found out that the house had been re-rated as an agricultural store – a fact that made our financial plight all the more desperate since it meant that we couldn't get any grant to restore the property.

INTRODUCTION

A HISTORY OF "PENY'S HEY"

Chapter Two
RENOVATION

There was much to be done. The house had been stripped of all signs of domestic use, so there were no hearths, no viable sinks, doors or windows, and no services in the house at all.

Pig pens had been built in the present sitting room:

Children had lit fires on the bedroom floors, and the roof was full of holes:

A survey revealed that the north wall of the single storey cottage (No.45) was bellying out, and there was damage to the top of the west gable on the two storey cottage (No.43). An architect took a quick look, said it needed "lots of money throwing at it", and declined further involvement! As we didn't have much money, it was clear that we would have to do as much of the work as possible ourselves. We did have some experience when, six years earlier, we'd bought a small back-to-back cottage in Almondbury and totally renovated it (with some notable blunders). After renting it out for some time, it was the sale of this cottage that then provided the capital to get on with the work at Hey.

We had some breathing space between the tender being accepted and the contracts finally being signed, and we took advantage of this to start clearing the site of as much of the many items of rubbish as possible. Everyone helped in our hour of need – including Andrea and Barrie in between university and work. We even squeezed half a freezing day of wall demolition in the stables from Stuart Dick – our first student lodger (taken in to help fund the project). Why demolish walls in stables when there's so much to do at the house itself? The answer is that the walls in the stables incorporated scaffolding poles – constituting the horizontal bars to the animal stalls – and we wanted these for subsequent work on the house. Waste and expense had to be minimised!

There had been no modern toilet arrangements, so our thoughts initially concentrated on the likelihood of having to install a septic tank – the excavations for which would have been quite prohibitive in depth and cost! Fortunately, we discovered that there was a surface water drain which connected to an existing 6" diameter salt glazed pipeline running from the top of the lane and joining the mains sewer at the bottom. Although there was doubt as to the ownership of this line, we were eventually able to prevail upon the water board to allow us to use it (though they weren't at all keen or helpful, and we really only succeeded by virtue of both water board and local authority in effect abdicating responsibility for the line). Even then, the building regulations inspectors took some persuading that the condition of the line was suitable for us to connect our soil system and use it as a sewer and surface water discharge combined, rather than just the latter. To make the connection, we had to dig a trench from the middle of the building line along the cleared area on the south side of the cottages, and under the dry stone perimeter wall. (Later on, the line had to be renewed right across under the lane, with a fresh connection into the main sewer at the other side of the lane.)

Electricity had been supplied in the mid 1950s to both house and barn, but had been disconnected and the installation condemned by the electricity board, insisting that it wasn't safe. There had also been a supply of town gas, but this was cut off when natural gas was piped to the area. At the time, the gas board had offered to install a pipeline to the nursery at the top of the lane free of charge, but unbelievably Geoff Whitelegg, the owner, turned the offer down! He was using oil to heat the greenhouses which was still cheaper than gas, as this was just before the 1970s oil crisis when oil prices rocketed. He's regretted that decision ever since. When we wanted to bring a new gas supply up the lane, the gas board were no longer touting for customers and quoted £500 – a figure which we just couldn't afford at that time – so we stuck with electricity.

Similarly, water had been piped to the property originally, but had been disconnected as the installation was not up to current standards. Some form of illegal flexible pipe had also been run to the 'tin barn' at the very top of the lane, but even this didn't provide water when we took over. There were two surface "springs" on the property – one by the "stables", the other just across from the door of the two-storey cottage. Although we didn't find out till later, there was also a proper well about 3ft across and 15ft deep alongside the north wall of the single-storey cottage. None of these were of use in providing water for the work in hand, so getting a proper supply of both water and electricity was the first top priority.

We had one small area on the property which we could make reasonably secure – this was the space under the stone stairs of 43, so we decided that we would bring services into the house at this point. Following family traditions, this has been known ever since as the 'bogey hole'. We fitted a new solid door and frame, with substantial padlock, and dug trenches to the north wall outside the bogey hole. For the electricity the trench only had a short distance to run directly from the pole at the edge of the property, but the trench for the water had to come from the lane. To guard against freezing, this had to be at least 30" deep to satisfy water board regulations. The ensuing excavations outside were difficult enough, but inside was extremely arduous as we had to work in the confined space of the bogey hole – only about 2ft square access – then chisel a hole through the foundation stonework at that depth, big enough to take two 4" diameter pipes: one for water; the other for electricity. As the north wall is 2'6" thick, this was no small task, but was eventually achieved, and the water supply was commissioned, along with just a simple switch box and power point sufficient to allow us to use power tools on site.

RENOVATION

The first architect we approached had declined the work, but luckily our son Jeff was working at the time for Hadwise, a building contractor, one of whose directors – Bill Bridgeman – had sufficient architectural expertise to draw up plans for us. His first suggestion was to extend the single storey cottage to meet the barn and incorporate the barn in the house. This seemed a bit grandiose for our means, and so the concept was changed to build a second storey on the single storey cottage and thus bring both cottages up to one two-storey level.

So the roof came off 45.

We were amazed at the size and weight of the stone slates, some of which were about 3' square and 2" thick – more like paving slabs than what you think of as roofing. To get them down, we used some corrugated iron sheets that were on site, as slides, supported by some spare timber joists (also on site,) and just slid them down these. Getting the purlins down was a major task as we didn't want to risk damaging the walls that were to stay. We erected a tower using scaffolding poles (again, largely with material that was already on site), and borrowed a set of chain blocks from Hepworth one weekend to lower the beams with. After much manoeuvring, Jeff, Dave and myself managed to get the beams onto the ground and muscle them out of the way using rollers, levers and shear brute force. Again, to save money and avoid waste, we planned to reuse as much of the existing timber on site as possible in the renovation.

Although Bill Bridgeman had been convinced that the north wall of the single storey cottage was sound, Kirklees Building Control thought otherwise and insisted that it had to be pulled down right to, and including, the foundation stones. The same applied to the internal wall separating what is now the kitchen and sitting room. The gable had to be taken down to eaves level, along with about 5ft of the whole height of the east wall at the corner with the north wall.

When the internal wall came down we exposed the "half height" cellar at the north end of what is now the kitchen. We had, right at the beginning, before any involvement with Building Control, seen that there was a "keeping" shelf in this cellar which in effect reduced the thickness of the north wall just below ground level, and tried to make this up to the same thickness as the rest of that wall with bricks. This was in the depth of winter, so we used mortar anti-freeze, but were very sceptical about the soundness of the work, and were rather relieved when we had to later undo it all! When demolishing the internal wall, we also removed all the stone flooring flags (saving for later reuse) and took out the few stone steps leading down into the cellar. The cellar had been partly filled in, and we dug it out so that we could completely fill it in solidly. Amongst the rubbish that we extracted was a very old rottenly rusted Villiers motor bike, and some tractor parts.

Dorothy Simmonds (about whom, more later) told us some years after this that when she lived at 43 in the 1920s, what is now the kitchen had been two bedrooms – one at the south side on the ground floor and the other at the opposite end up three or four stairs. This seems to have been over the cellar, and was probably lit by the small window high in the wall that was still there when we took on the property. It's possible that the cellar was only half below ground because of the difficulty in excavating through the solid shale rock that the house stands on.

Adjoining the east gable had been an Anderson corrugated iron air raid shelter, still concreted into the ground, as it had been for the second world war. This was demolished early on in the work. Finally, all that was left standing of the single storey cottage was the south wall and part of the east gable. Removing the foundation stones of the north wall left us with the quandary of how to cope with the open well, which turned out to be just under where the new foundations had to go. Fortunately, we had some positive guidance from Building Control, suggesting a reinforced concrete cap over the well, integrated with the concrete for the foundations, which is what we did.

One of the major battles with Kirklees bureaucracy was over the construction of the new north wall. They originally insisted on coursed natural stone. This would have been prohibitively expensive for us, as well as being more difficult to build than using concrete blocks, which was our preference. We eventually had a "site meeting" with officers from the planning department who reluctantly accepted our arguments. We contended that, since the north wall of the two-storey cottage was well weathered and beyond any discernible "coursing", butting new coursed stonework straight up to it would not be as visually acceptable as rendering throughout. Rendering would protect the existing decayed stone and would also match the existing rendering on the west gable.

Having won the battle of the north wall, we were then able to press on with rebuilding. The foundations and walls took shape relatively quickly with much help from Jeff, ably assisted by Dave, who did sterling work in mixing mortar and keeping us supplied with materials.

Although the east gable doorway was to remain, it was too low for modern building regulations, so we took off the lintel and increased the height by adding two stones above the existing stone jambs. We were able to retain the original iron hinges and sneck which are leaded into the stone jambs. The sneck is shaped to accommodate the large wooden bolt that would have secured the original door. The door in the south wall was similarly equipped, but the sneck had been sawn off.

Building off new foundations on the north wall proved relatively easy compared with trying to fit an 11" cavity wall on the existing 2ft thick solid rubble walls on the south and east, where special provision had to be made to span the existing wall thickness sufficiently to take the weight of the rest of the increased wall height. A further complication arose in having to integrate damp proof course PVC to form a cavity tray over the change in wall thickness, which itself had to change to an 11" cavity wall at the north corner. Ventilation / drainage slots also had to be provided in the outer skin, and provision made for galvanised tie bars on the inner leaf. Mistakes were made, but we persevered, and were even able to add our own little eccentricities like re-using the wall plate from the south wall, in its original position, but turned through 90° to show the cut-outs for the rafters (and no longer supporting the roof, of course).

To span the sitting room we had to provide additional support for the first floor joists. Again, we were able to reuse timber that we'd taken from the roof, and fitted one of the roof purlins across the sitting room to support the joists. There was a bit of doubt about the strength of this beam, because although it is good solid seasoned oak it reduces quite a bit in section towards one end. To alleviate this, we took yet another beam recovered from the roof as a supporting upright, creating in the process something of a fairly unusual feature for the sitting room.

CHAPTER THREE
EARLY RECORDS ABOUT HEY

The name "Hey" derives from an Old English word "aeg", meaning an enclosure, usually associated with animals. Throughout its history, Hey is described as pastureland, and cows are still grazed there today. The wetness of the land is vividly reflected in the eighteenth century naming of the close nearest the wood as "The Pudding Close" – an old term for a wet area.

In front of Hey lay the large open field of Birchenley, which included all the present-day fields between Hey and Kaye Lane. In medieval times, and maybe before, this field would be sown with arable crops, and perhaps its proximity to the Hey may have led to the first enclosure, in order to separate the animals from the crops.

Around the house and garden are several elder trees. The elder has historic associations with human occupation, and long ago it was customary to plant an elder tree close to a new house, so the presence of these trees confirms early human settlement on the site. The tree was valued for its magical and medicinal properties and was carefully tended by successive residents, though elder wood was never used to make a bed, as it would be certain to bring bad dreams to the sleeper! Judas Iscariot, according to tradition, hanged himself from an elder tree. People still come to pick the elderberries to make home-brewed wine.

After the Norman Conquest, the Manor of Almondbury was held by the De Laci family for about 300 years, eventually passing by marriage to the Earl of Lancaster. He rebelled against his cousin King Edward II, and was executed and his estates confiscated by the crown. In 1372 the Manor became part of the Duchy of Lancaster when John of Gaunt, a younger son of Edward III, was created Duke of Lancaster and given the traitorous Earl's lands. When John of Gaunt's son became Henry IV, Almondbury became a royal manor and was owned by the king!

"Hey" stands on a steep hillside overlooking the village school in Lowerhouses, Huddersfield. A clue to its age lies in its situation. As with most old Yorkshire houses, it is on an east-west axis with blind gables into the prevailing winds, and most of its windows on the south facing front. This front faces an old field path from Longley, and the house has its back to a village unimagined when first it was built! It was originally an agricultural area, enclosed about six hundred years ago. Four hundred years ago it had become a small settlement within the Manor of Almondbury, and two hundred years later it had grown into a small hamlet. Nowadays it has been swallowed up by the nearby village of Lowerhouses, and is remembered only in the street name Hey Lane, although in an old plan of 1872, the present Hey Lane is named "Occupation Rd" – a name often applied to a road with no existing name.

In the sixteenth and seventeenth centuries, Hey looked out over a network of fields where Lowerhouses now stands, and Longley and Kidroyd were its nearest neighbours. Lowerhouses did not evolve as a village until the nineteenth century. Before then it was referred to as Nether or Far Longley, and Hey Lane itself was only constructed in the late 18th century.

In the Inquisition into the Manor of Almondbury of 1340, Thomas Wood of Longley, a direct forbear of John, holds six acres as tenant-at-will somewhere in the vicinity of Longley. Possibly this is the very first reference to Hey. The reasons for believing this are as follows: firstly, the owner is a member of the Wood family which owned Hey until 1538, and lived close by; secondly, it was always held on the lesser tenant-at-will basis; and finally, all the inquisitions up to 1584 describe Hey as 6 acres.

In 1380 William Wood held Hey, and the poll tax taken in that year described him as a wright or carpenter. He paid 6d in tax, putting him well below a prosperous farmer, who would have paid 1s–2s. (Earls were charged at £4). As a wright, his work would have included framing up wooden buildings in his yard before they were erected on site.

The Hey and the Hey Green are both first actually mentioned by name in the next inquisition into the Manor of Almondbury in 1425. This suggests that the Hey had been in existence for some time before that, as it had given the common land its particular name of Hey Green. It is described in the 1425 survey as an area of six acres, held as a tenant-at-will by John Wood of Longley. Before 1425 it had formed part of the glebe, the tenant being the "Parson at Almanburie".

Rents generally hadn't changed since 1340, and land was still 4d an acre. Hey, however, was now rented out at 5s 1d a year – the highest rent of any property in the manor held on a tenant-at-will basis. This steep rise in rent, from 2s 2d a year in 1340, coupled with the fact that in this period a carpenter held the property, and the presence of timbers from an original timber-framed house, surely point to the first house on this site being built in the late 14th century – probably a farmhouse and outbuildings. Perhaps William built it for a son or daughter.

The rents paid in this period are interesting:

- 1340:
    — Robert Wood ~ 15½ acres ~ 5s 2d
    — Thomas Wood ~ 6 acres ~ 2s 2d
- 1425:
    — John Wood ~ 15½ acres ~ 5s 2d
    — John Wood, Hey ~ 6 acres ~ 5s 1d
- 1584:
    — John Ramsden ~ 15½ acres ~ 5s 2d
    — John Ramsden, Hey, Messuage ~ 6 acres ~ 5s 1d

It's worth mentioning that, at 5s 1d, the rent is the highest paid by any tenant-at-will. The survey carried out in 1584 lists Hey as a messuage (a house with associated outbuildings). The rent, though, is still 5s 1d – no inflation in those days! As the rent is the same in 1425 and 1584, and as there is definitely a house on the site in 1584, the logical conclusion seems to be that there was also a house on the site in 1425. Assuming that the six acres referred to are the same (which seems very likely), then a great change has taken place between 1340 and 1425, at a time when other rents in the area were stable. The probable cause seems to be the building of a house and outbuildings.

CHAPTER FOUR
OWNERSHIP OF HEY

Hey began as part of the Manor of Almondbury, which was owned by the Crown. The tenants were the Wood family of Longley until the death of John Wood in 1538. He was the last of the male line, and his property within the Manor of Almondbury was acquired by his son-in-law, William Ramsden. In 1627 Sir John Ramsden bought the Manor of Almondbury and Hey became part of the Ramsden Estate. In 1933 Huddersfield Corporation bought the Ramsden Estate, and Hey became municipally owned.

A slow decline at Hey had begun at the beginning of the 19th century, when the land associated with Hey had shrunk to 11 acres. By the middle of the 19th century, the houses and land were totally separate, although pigs and hens were kept in the garden well into the 20th century. By the middle of the 20th century the houses were so run down that they had become uninhabitable. At this point, the people moved out and the animals moved in! All the internal fittings were removed to accommodate pens for the animals; the roof leaked; and the walls bulged.

In 1985, the successor to Huddersfield Corporation, Kirklees Council, sold the property into private ownership, and the house underwent a period of sympathetic restoration, to become, once again, a dwelling fit for people. Today, totally renovated, it proudly stands once more overlooking the village of Lowerhouses, occupying the prominent position as it has for nearly six centuries.

Chapter Five
TENANTS AT HEY

Pre-1425	—	The Parson at Almanburie
1425	—	John Wood of Longley
1542	—	William Ramsden
(1562)	—	John Wood of Hey
(1576)	—	John Wood of Hey
(1579)	—	John Wood of Hey
(1584)	—	John Wood of Hey
1634	—	William Wimpeny
1605	—	William Peny
1716	—	James Haigh
Pre-1741	—	Joseph Wimpenny
1741	—	Thomas Heaton
1766	—	Joshua Beaumont
1780	—	Joseph Brooke
1797	—	?
1805–1820	—	John Bagguley
1820–1831	—	William Kaye, Greenwood
1823	—	George Blackburn, Mary North
1832	—	William Kaye
1841–1850	—	John Brook
1851	—	Samuel Cocker
1865–1884	—	Anthony Knowles Kaye
1871	—	Richard Beaumont
1884	—	Joseph Knowles Kaye

The first mention of Hey in 1425 tells us that the previous tenant was "the parson at Almanburie", and the present tenant was John Wood of Longley. The Wood family sub-let the property, and the first sub-tenant traceable is a man also called John Wood, who lived at Hey, and was married at Almondbury Parish Church on July 5th 1562 to Helen Sampson. (This is an unusual name locally, and the only family of this name is recorded in the Hartshead Parish Register – living by Kirklees Mill in the early 17th century.)

John and Helen had eight children – four boys and four girls, three of whom died in infancy. Helen died in childbirth in 1579, and in 1580 John married his second wife, Jane Dyson. Jane came from a family living nearby at Hole Bottom, and had been godmother to the Wood's daughter Isabel. John himself died in 1588, followed by his wife in 1590. He seems to have been a respected member of the community, and he and his wife frequently stood as godparents to the children of neighbouring families. John was sufficiently influential as to have William Ramsden senior and his nephew, also William, stand as godfathers to his son William in 1566.

In March 1576, Sibella Nettleton, wife of Robert Nettleton and a cousin of William Ramsden of Longley, stood as godmother to John Wood's son Richard. In the Parish Register, on August 26th 1576, a special note tells us that John Wood of Hey attended the funeral of Edmund Hoyle, who had died in London. John had business dealings with Edmund, and they jointly held the tenancy of a messuage from the Ramsden Estate. In addition, John also held the tenancy of the East Birchinleyfield, a field created from part of the large open field mentioned previously, which was very close to Hey.

By 1542, William Ramsden had acquired all the land formerly belonging to his father-in-law, John Wood. This included Hey, and several references are made to "John Wood of Hey" in William's estate papers. In 1570/71, for instance, there is a memorandum to the effect that:

> "John Wodde of the Hey must pay xxv s. of midsomer day 1571 for five shepe which John Blagburne had the xviii day of January."

On June 24th 1579 there is an item "lent to John Wood of Hey – 30 li [shillings]", and the Manorial Survey of 1584 notes that:

> "John Wodd of the Hey tenant to John Ramsden Gent. hath encroached upon the waste 5d of the Hey Green a certain parcel containing by estimation an acre and a half."

Possibly this Wood family were a junior branch of the Wood family at Longley Hall, surviving in Longley after the main branch failed due to the lack of a male heir; or perhaps John Wood was a grandson of John Wood of Longley by his illegitimate son, George.

TENANTS AT HEY

By 1605, the Wimpenny family were living at Hey. At the baptism of their third child (a daughter, Anna), her father is recorded as "William Wimpeny of Hay". They were a local family, well known to John Wood of Hey. At the baptism of Hugonis Ramsden's daughter Jane on April 4th 1568, Helen Wood – John Wood's wife – and Gilbert Penye were both godparents. Gilbert Wimpeny, William's father, was the tenant of a house built "within living memory" (of the 1584 survey) on land owned by John Appleyard, who held land and tenements at Longley.

William Senior's famous map of the township of Almondbury, drawn in 1634, depicts a house on the same site as the present house, and describes it as "Wm Peny his hey". The fields around Hey, extending to some 30 acres, were also shown as belonging to William Peny, including a "spring" of wood, known as "Cate Spring". In time his family was to give its name to this wood, and it became the present day Penny Spring Wood.

Almondbury Manor Court records in 1741 that Joseph Wimpenny had only recently ceased to be the tenant of Hey, and the Parish Registers record Wimpenys at the Hey to the end of the 17th century. It seems possible that the family association could have lasted for well over 100 years.

In 1623/24, William Wimpenny was constable of Almondbury, and his report and statement of accounts are preserved amongst the Ramsden papers in the archives at Huddersfield library. The Wimpenny family is still at Hey in 1681, when Joseph Wimpenny's daughter Mary was baptised. Twins are recorded every generation for three generations. In 1688 a spinster from Hey, with the surname Wimpenny was buried in Almondbury. Between 1676 and 1681 Joseph Wimpenny of Hey has three children: William; Joseph; and Mary. His son Joseph is recorded in the Almondbury Court Rolls as having recently given up the tenancy of Hey in 1741, and Thomas Heaton has just taken possession.

The Ramsden estate map drawn by Timothy Oldfield in 1716 shows the house, and the estate survey lists the tenant as James Haigh. The next clear reference is to a tenant in 1766. His name was Joshua Beaumont, and his holding around the Hey was 28 acres, including the aptly named Pudding Close. His rent was 12s 6d for the house, and £8 4s 0d for the land. Luke Beaumont holds less land, at 22 acres, the majority described as pasture, and by 1780 Joseph Brooke was paying £1 for the house and barn, and £13 12s for 16 acres of land. It is in this survey that the house is first described as a "house in two dwellings". In 1807, a Thomas Brook is paying 5s rent for a cottage at Hey – perhaps this is Joseph's son.

In 1775 Hey expanded when John Boothroyd built himself a house and barn further up the hill from the original Hey. Henceforward at least two tenants, and sometimes four, are resident at what has become a small hamlet. This new farmhouse passed down through the same family, and the Boothroyd family were still living there in 1861. In 1794 the Parish Constable for Almondbury is John Boothroyd. After a gap of 170 years, perhaps the office has returned to Hey!

The Ramsden Estate appears to have been managed with some sympathy and flexibility at this time, and so in 1780 John Boothroyd had £9 10s of his rent of £11 2s 6d abated "on account of great improvements I land and buildings at his own expense". In 1797 the widow of Thomas Sykes at Hey had £4 of her rent abated "on account of her being a widow with three small children and having her brother, who is a caitiff to support". (Caitiff is a Yorkshire dialect word for someone who is long term sick.) This still left her with £22 to pay, plus £1 15s interest on a loan of £30 to build a barn. The land still extended to 16 acres at this time, and it was at this point that the Ramsden Estate divided the house into two, leaving the widow and her family with a much smaller house.

From Candlemas in 1805 a new tenant took over at the original Hey. His name was John Bagguley, and he stayed until 1820. He rented 11 acres, and in 1805 paid 3s land tax – the first mention of any tax (the French wars against Napoleon were proving expensive). With this tax the rent was £16, and the house and barn were a further £2 10s. As John Boothroyd only paid 5s for his house and barn, this seems rather expensive, but throughout its history the Hey seems to have commanded a high rent in comparison with other properties.

The next tenancy was a partnership between William Kaye and someone called Greenwood. Kaye and Greenwood continued as tenants until 1831 when William Kaye alone took over. Between 1840 and 1844 he acquired a dyehouse in Smithy Lane, and by 1848 a distillery is mentioned there, plus a gasworks! Joshua Kaye took over the business and in 1874 Anthony Kaye sold his gasworks at Moldgreen to the new Borough Council for £17,000. The Directory for 1845 has this entry:

"KAYE – JOSHUA (AQUAFORTIS AND SPIRIT OF SALTS) MOLDGREEN"

In 1865 Anthony Knowles Kaye rents Hey – the land being described as "fine land", and in February 1884 Joseph Knowles Kaye takes over. William Kaye, by now described as a man of independent means, aged 65, is living with his wife and a female servant in Smithy Lane. Joshua Kaye, a manufacturing chemist, is also living at Smithy Lane with his wife and three children. Their household also boasts a servant – a fifteen year old girl called Mary Dyson. Although the tenancy passes down through the Kaye family they themselves are obviously not resident at Hey.

There is a record in April 1822 to the effect that "James Sykes of Hey buries still born child". In 1823 a daughter Betty was born to George Blackburn and Mary North at Hey, and in 1825 another daughter, Hannah, arrived. George Blackburn was a clothier and presumably lived in the double storey cottage with its upper floor well lit by mullion windows and ideal for a loom and weaving. The barnyard went with the tenancy of the single storey cottage, and in 1837 Charlotte Redgate of Hey in Almondbury presented her husband John with a baby daughter christened Martha. Her father was described as a farmer.

It is interesting to note that a linen draper called Samuel Knowles also lives in Smithy Lane in this period. Possibly Joshua Kaye married his daughter, since Knowles is incorporated into the names of succeeding generations of Kayes.

In 1841 the houses at Hey are sublet to a fancy weaver called John Brook, along with his wife and eight children, and an agricultural labourer called John Herring, with his wife and three children. Further up the hill are John Boothroyd, a stone mason, with his wife and family, and an elderly married couple named Sykes, who are farmers.

By 1851 John Brook has gone, and Samuel Cocker, a handloom weaver, has moved in with his wife, Hannah, who is a bobbin winder, and their five-year-old daughter Sarah. In 1844 Samuel had been lodging with Hannah Boothroyd at her alehouse in Lowerhouses. By this time, Mary Herring is a widow, and is also working as a bobbin winder, as is her daughter, Clara. Mary Ann, the younger girl, is a milliner. Up the hill the Sykes have gone, and John Boothroyd's family are the only residents. His eldest daughter now has an illegitimate son aged four living with the family.

In 1861 Samuel Cocker has abandoned his handloom weaving in favour of fancy weaving, and Mary Herring's house is occupied by a farm labourer called William Charlesworth. He is 62 and lives with his daughter and granddaughter. At the Boothroyd's, John's wife has died, and he has remarried. In addition to his work as stone mason, he now farms 6 acres as well.

None of the residents at Hey seem to stay long, and by 1871 another family is resident. Richard Beaumont is there and is described as an engine maker. He is a married man with 3 sons and 3 daughters aged from 9 months to 16 years old. No other family is mentioned. After almost 100 years, the Boothroyds have left Hey Farm, and a builder, Mark Sykes, is living there with their 2 sons and 2 daughters. In 1878 he builds a new cottage adjoining the original one.

CHAPTER SIX
ARCHITECTURE OF THE HOUSE

It wasn't until we'd had chance to settle in and get decorations done that, after many deliberations by ourselves and visitors, who mostly speculated that the old oak beams must have originated as ships' timbers, we thought enough about the issue to ask expert advice. Mr. David Mitchelmore was contacted (he owned a firm in Horbury that specialised in renovating old structures for such prestigious buildings as Castle Howard). He identified much of the timber as mediaeval in origin, some he thought were purlins with slots cut to fit wind braces from a cruck framed house possibly dating from the 13th century. These can now be seen in the beams in the sitting room and kitchen.

In the beginning...

It was Mr. Mitchelmore's opinion that although there had probably been several rebuilds, all had been on the original foundations. My own theories are as follows:

As the house appears on the 1716 map (gable at 43 facing South, gable at 45 facing East), it could have been an open hall, with parlour and chamber over in a low gable at the West end., the plan being L shaped, with the L on its side and the base aligned on a North - South axis. In 1780 great changes occurred to make the house become two. The West gable was rebuilt and enlarged. The evidence for this can be seen in the completely different stonework from the rest of the house. In addition, the crow steps (stones protruding from the gable to throw water from the join with the roof of the single storey cottage) are typically 18th century. The stone shelf in the main bathroom is one of the original crows steps left in place. Similarly, the different styles of joists in the dining room suggest a re-use of substantial 16th century chamfered ones being augmented by some of inferior quality - again also suggesting an enlargement of the building. The fact that the old joists sit atop pitch pine beams proves that the rebuilding was from the ground up, as imported pine only arrived in Huddersfield after the building of the canal in 1775 made it possible. The colour of the stonework and the narrow courses match the original building at Hey Farm (1775), and some of the cottages down Lowerhouses Lane, which date from the beginning of the 19th century. Many of the remains of the old stone field walls show that they too were built of similar stone.

Stone is a heavy and costly material to transport, and in the past was only used in ordinary buildings if there was a local supply. We know from old maps that there were three quarries in the area of Longley, all now unrecognisable. There was one at Ashenhurst at the back of Russet Grove, just above Whitegate Road, and it is just possible to see the outline of the edge of the quarry if you know where to look. The one at the top of Fanny Moor is still known locally as the old quarry, but the one nearest to Hey lay on the edge of Lowerhouses Lane across from St Mary's Church, and the site now of a modern bungalow. It would make a lot of sense to use stone from that quarry to build at Hey and Lowerhouses.

John Boothroyd was a stonemason and is known to have built Hey Farm. It seems at least possible that he or his son, who was also a stonemason, was also involved with these other similar buildings at Hey. The cottage down Lowerhouses Lane with the Brewers sign over the lintel has the same stone and narrow courses, and was the original Mason's Arms pub, which the records show was built and named by the Boothroyd family in 1814.

Returning to Hey: the West gable had been enlarged re-using much of the original timber, especially in the roof, where most of the beams show signs of re-use. Some carry the groove originally cut to hold wattle and daub infill. A chimney was built with handmade bricks against the gable wall, and the connecting door was filled in. This door had been re-opened when we bought the property, but ex-residents who have visited have no memory of it. Quite recently an old doorway has been discovered at Longley Old Hall, whose construction matches our doorway. The doorway at the Hall is directly under a first floor doorway which dates from the 14th century, but whether this carries any significance for ours is difficult to say.

Both of the cottages at Hey formed by the 1780 alterations had lean-to wash kitchens, a place for ashes, and an outside earth closet. All these buildings except the west cottage earth closet had gone by the time we came, but they had originally completely closed the house off from the field at the back. To access the well alongside the north wall there was a gate between the wash kitchen of the east cottage and its earth closet and ashpit. This well was the only source of water for the cottages until after the second world war. There was a small 3ft deep well across from the front door of the west cottage, which we've been told was used for washing water, but all drinking water had to be fetched in a bucket from the well on the north wall. The position of this well may suggest that there was a pump from it into the east cottage – an arrangement that I know existed at an old farm I knew as a child.

Both outside doors to the cottages date from 1780, with identical iron door furniture, that in the east cottage surviving more intact than the other. This is possibly because the west cottage was inhabited for longer, and had a more modern door fitted. The house had originally been built along the traditional east-west alignment common in old Yorkshire houses, with blind gables (i.e. no openings), small windows on the north side, and door and main windows on the south. As the prevailing wind is from the west, and in bitter weather from the east, it makes good sense to have no openings on these sides to let in the draughts! Pity, then, poor widow Sykes who suddenly found herself with an east facing door directly into her only living room. It would have been a bit sheltered by the barn, but nevertheless, with the ill-fitting doors of the time, it must have been very cold. I think the front door would originally have been where the present front kitchen window is.

The long narrow kitchen had me puzzled for quite a while. From 1780 until that cottage was abandoned it formed two bedrooms, each with a door from the living/kitchen, although the room at the north end was up three or four stairs in order to accommodate the half cellar beneath, and I imagine was unceiled. The door from the present kitchen to the sitting room was the door into this back bedroom, and alongside it was the door to the cellar. When we first took over the house, there was a square opening high in the dividing wall between the present kitchen and sitting room leading into the roof space over the front bedroom. Perhaps extra children curled up here. I think originally the long narrow kitchen was partly the entrance passage and partly a large open fireplace.

Sitting room

The extremely strong (and of course extensively seasoned!) cruck beams were used as the main supports for the upper floors in the sitting room and kitchen. They were recovered from the previous single storey cottage roof. The peg holes show where the rafters were attached and the mortices bear witness to the positions of wind braces attaching the purlin to the main crucks.

The supporting upright beam still has bark on it, and so may originally have been used in an agricultural building. (The barn on site dated from 1780, but there were farm buildings here from at least 1560.)

The north wall of the sitting room was rebuilt in 1986 and the window close to the east gable was replaced by the present larger stone mullioned window. The west light of this window is now over the position of the 5m deep stone-lined well immediately alongside the foundations (now capped with reinforced concrete).

Hinges and bolt bracket and sneck have been retained at the outside door, though the doorway itself had to be heightened in 1986 to comply with modern building regulations.

The wall plate on the south wall is re-used from virtually its original 1780 position, but turned on edge to reveal the rafters notches.

Kitchen

Over the doorway from the sitting room into the kitchen is the header from a medieval oriel window – a window with 5 lights with oak mullions – never used with glass. We turned this on edge to show the grooves for the reveals and the mortices for the wooden mullions. The doorway connecting the kitchen with the present dining room must have been opened up some time after the two cottages ceased to be lived in, though it seems likely to have existed before the 1780 division of the house, judging by the age and configuration of the oak lintels and stone jambs.

The north wall of the kitchen had to be demolished in the 1986 restoration, and the small window high in the wall was replaced by the present more traditionally sized and positioned window. In the original structure at this point was a "half-depth" cellar and a mezzanine floor over.

At the south end of the kitchen, the wall plate is re-used from very close to its original position, but again turned over to show the notches to take the ends of the rafters. Also on this wall we retained the character of the 1780 construction by keeping the window seat.

Dining room

The dining room ceiling joists were dated by the style of the spoke shave chamfer as being 16th century.

The pine beams date from the 1780 reconstruction, having been imported via the then "new" canal. Running along the whole length of the south wall of the dining room and extending as a lintel over the outside door is an oak beam with a top rebate and mortice and peg holes – evidence of its previous use in a different location.

The wall separating the dining room and kitchen has had emulsion painted over the stonework to reflect its earlier limewashed appearance. The oak lintel and padstones in this wall have again been retained from the 1780 reconstruction. The chains, shears and horseshoes adorning the dining room are all articles recovered during the restoration work in 1986.

Structured to represent a vernacular inglenook, the dining room fireplace was built in hand made Georgian bricks that we recovered from the 1780 chimney breast in the room above, so they've moved very little from their original site. The fireplace lintel is an oak purlin recovered from the roof of the adjoining single-storey cottage. Yorkshire stone slabs from the original stone floor in this room form the present hearth.

First floor

Upstairs, exposed roof timbers have grooves where upright staves were slotted in as the uprights for wattle and daub walls. One of these timbers is a bridging beam for an upper floor, with clear evidence of the holes cut to take the joists. The groove ends about 1 metre from the end of the beam, and it is thought that this may have been where the staircase was.

North staircase

This stone staircase dates from the restructuring of 1780. The third riser is slightly higher than the others, and marks where there was once a door. Initially, the first floor would have been completely open, with the handloom between the two south facing windows. The later creation of two bedrooms resulted in the staircase receiving no light at all – the staircase downstairs having solid walls up both sides. As a child, Mrs Dorothy Simmonds found it quite frightening.

The stair door was gone by the time we arrived, but we added the stairs window for extra light. Mr David Mitchelmore identified the timber we put as the lintel as part of an oriel window – i.e. a window that jutted out from the oak frame. The original timber was much longer and had five cut-outs where now only two are visible.

Dorothy Simmonds also described the stair door as one with a latch only on the kitchen side of the door. When coming down the stairs it had to be operated by pushing a finger through a hole provided. Knowing the darkness frightened her, one of her older brothers would grab hold of her finger if he saw it coming through the door, making her even more scared.

APPENDIX
DENDROCHRONOLOGY REPORT

Nottingham Tree-Ring Dating Laboratory

Dendrochronology, timber analysis, and historic building consultants

Tree-ring analysis of timbers from:

"Peny's Hey", 43 Hey Lane
Lowerhouses
Huddesrfield
West Yorkshire

A. J. Arnold
R. E. Howard
M. Hurford

With an historical introduction by Patricia Dyson

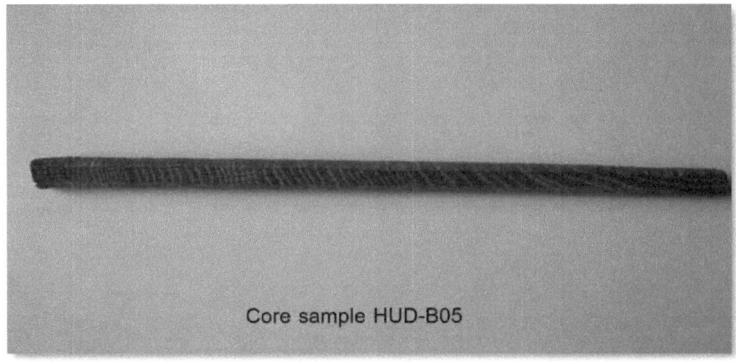

Core sample HUD-B05

Summary

Analysis by dendrochronology of samples from 10 different oak beams in this house suggest that at least two, and possibly three, phases of felling are represented in the timbers found here.

The earliest timbers, comprising ground floor ceiling beams, a post, and a fireplace bressummer, were probably all felled in 1481. Later timbers, represented by roof beams and a ground-floor lintel, were possibly felled c.1580.

A single site chronology, HUDBSQ01, comprising seven samples can be produced from the analysed samples, its 188 rings spanning the years 1386–1573. Three other samples remain undated.

Historical introduction

The House, Peny's Hey, stands on a shale outcrop overlooking the village of Longley, about one mile south-east of Huddersfield, in West Yorkshire; it is so called because it appears on William Senior's map of 1634 as "William Peny – his Hey" (Fig 1). In the past, Longley was part of the Manor of Almondbury, which in turn takes its name from the nearby Iron Age fort, and is the original hilltop village that pre-dates Huddersfield.

The Manor of Almondbury formed part of the Honour of Pontefract, which William the Conqueror gifted to Ilbert de Laci. The De Laci heiress eventually married Thomas, Earl of Lancaster, and after his rebellion in 1322 the Manor was sequestered to the Crown, eventually becoming part of the Duchy of Lancaster, part of the English Monarch's personal holdings. The Ramsden family purchased the manor from the Crown in 1627.

The earliest recorded tenants at Hey were the Wood family. They first appeared in Longley in 1330 when Robert Wood witnessed a Deed. This family prospered in Longley for the next 200 years. In 1523 a taxation roll of Henry VIII assessed John Wood of Longley at £10, which made him the richest man in Almondbury. In 1530 John Wood disowned his son and sensing a business opportunity Robert Ramsden married his son William to one of John Wood's daughters. Eventually, William Ramsden acquired all of his father-in-law's estates within the manor, including Hey. Thus, in 600 years, Hey was held by just 2 families.

"Hey" comes from the Old English word "Aeg", meaning an enclosure, and at Peny's Hey this enclosure was historically 6 acres. The suffix "ley", as in "Longley", means a clearing, and both names pre-date the Norman Conquest.

Between 1340 and 1584 three inquisitions (enquiries into land tenure and rents) were held into the Manor of Almondbury. Rent details from these surveys show a pattern which could be taken to indicate the building of a house on the site sometime after 1340:

- 1340:
    — Robert Wood ~ 15½ acres ~ 5s 2d
    — Thomas Wood ~ 6 acres ~ 2s 2d
- 1425:
    — John Wood ~ 15½ acres ~ 5s 2d
    — John Wood, Hey ~ 6 acres ~ 5s 1d
- 1584:
    — John Ramsden ~ 15½ acres ~ 5s 2d
    — John Ramsden, Hey, Messuage ~ 6 acres ~ 5s 1d

It will be seen that while, between 1340 and 1425, the rent of the 15½ acres remains the same, that for the 6 acres rises sharply, implying some change here. It will further be seen that between 1425 and 1584 the rent for both the "Hey" and the 15½ acres remain static, i.e. there has been no change during those years. As the 1584 inquisition describes Hey as a "messuage" (a house and outbuildings), it is probable that the messuage has been there since at least 1425 – hence the big increase in rent by that time.

After 1584, Peny's Hey is shown on two estate maps drawn in 1634 and 1716, and appears continuously in the Ramsden Estate Rentals up until 1920 when the estate, amounting to some 4,300 acres, was acquired by Huddersfield Corporation.

The house

From 1920 onwards, the house (Figure 2) suffered indifferent neglect, and by 1985 it was officially unfit for habitation, and home to pigs. The present owners' subsequent restoration was therefore radical, and exposed the bare bones of the building. The presence of a number of large oak timbers showing signs of specific earlier use was sufficiently intriguing to prompt professional advice from an expert in timber framed buildings, in this instance, David Michelmore. He identified a "wealth of medieval timbers" and suggested the following phasing:

1. A timber framed house – evidenced by purlins with cut-outs for wind braces, and the header from an oak-mullioned window.

2. A complete rebuild in stone in the sixteenth century – which

he deduced from chamfered and stopped ceiling joists typical of that period, reused during the eighteenth century in what is now the dining room.

3. The Ramsden Estate Rental for 1780 states that the house has been divided and Mr Michelmore found evidence to indicate that the western end of the house had been completely reconstructed. Beams in the ground floor room are of imported pine, tying in well with the opening of the Huddersfield Canal in 1775. As previously mentioned, the pine beams are used in conjunction with the much older oak joists. The roof construction in this part of the house is typically eighteenth century, being of queen post with tusked tenon purlins, some showing signs of earlier use as they are grooved to take wattle and daub panels.

The timbers

The timbers presently within Peny's Hey comprise what are now single oak bridging beams (they may originally have been purlins and are reused here) to two of the ground-floor ceilings, that of the living room and the kitchen (at the east end and middle of the building respectively), as well as a series of door and window lintels, wall plates or posts. There is also a bressummer to the fireplace in the dining room at the west end of the house (Figs 3a–c). To the upper floors the timbers comprise a single principal rafter truss with tiebeam, vertical queen posts, and diagonal struts, at the west end of the building, there also being single purlins to each pitch of the roof at the west end (Figs 4a–b). A number of these timbers showed evidence, by way of redundant mortices and pegholes, of having been salvaged and reused in their present position. All the roof timbers to the middle and east end of the house are modern replacements.

Not all the oak timbers were suitable for tree-ring dating, being derived from fast-grown trees which were unlikely to provide samples with sufficient rings for reliable analysis, i.e. with more than 54 rings. There were, in addition to the oak, a small number of pine timbers, most notably the two ceiling beams to the dining room, and timbers to the south window of the kitchen. Samples were not taken from such timbers.

Sampling

Sampling and analysis by tree-ring dating of the timbers within Peny's Hey were commissioned by the owners, Mr and Mrs Dyson. This was undertaken out of personal interest and concern for the building, and as part of a general programme of research in to its history and development.

It was realised, however, that some of the timbers showed little structural integrity, that is they were not all jointed and pegged together to form a coherent structural frame, and that many of them showed signs, by way of redundant mortices and pegholes, of previous use, and as such might not necessarily be related directly to the present building. Despite this it was hoped that tree-ring dating, in conjunction with the structural and stylistic interpretation undertaken by David Michelmore, and the documentary evidence unearthed by Mrs Pat Dyson, that some further information might be deduced from tree-ring analysis.

Thus, from the oak timbers available a total of 10 samples were obtained by coring. Each sample was given the code HUD-B (for Huddersfield, site "B") and numbered 01–10. The positions of these samples are marked on a sketch plan made at the time of sampling, worked-up to that given in Figures 6a–b. Details of the samples are given in Table 1. In this Table the frames, beams and individual timbers have been located and numbered on a north-south or east-west basis as appropriate.

Tree-ring dating

Tree-ring dating relies on a few simple, but quite fundamental, principles. Firstly, as is commonly known, trees (particularly oak trees, the most frequently used building timber in England) grow by adding one, and only one, growth-ring to their circumference each, and every, year. Each new annual growth-ring is added to the outside of the previous year's growth just below the bark. The width of this annual growth-ring is largely, though not exclusively, determined by the weather conditions during the growth period (roughly March – September). In general, good conditions produce wider rings and poor conditions produce narrower rings. Thus, over the lifetime of a tree, the annual growth-rings display a climatically influenced pattern. Furthermore, and importantly, all trees growing in the same area at the same time will be influenced by the same growing conditions and the annual growth-rings of all of them will respond in a similar, though not identical, way.

Secondly, because the weather over any number of consecutive years is unique, so too is the growth-ring pattern of the tree. The pattern of a short period of growth, 20, 30 or even 40 consecutive years, might conceivably be repeated two or even three times in the last one thousand years. A short pattern might also be repeated at different time periods in different parts of the country because of differences in regional micro-climates. It is less likely, however, that such problems would occur with the pattern of a longer period of growth, that is, anything in excess of 54 years or so. In essence, a short period of growth, anything less than 54 rings, is not reliable, and the longer the period of time under comparison the better.

The third principle of tree-ring dating is that, until the early to mid-nineteenth century, builders of timber-framed houses usually obtained all the wood needed for a given structure by felling the necessary trees in a single operation from one patch of woodland, or from closely adjacent woods. Furthermore, and contrary to popular belief, the timber was used "green" and without seasoning, and there was very little long-term storage as in timber-yards of today. This fact has been well established from a number of studies where tree-ring dating has been undertaken in conjunction with documentary studies. Thus, establishing the felling date for a group of timbers gives a very precise indication of the date of their use in a building.

Tree-ring dating relies on obtaining the growth pattern of trees from sample timbers of unknown date by measuring the width of the annual growth-rings. This is done to a tolerance of 1/100 of a millimetre. The growth patterns of these samples of unknown date are then compared with a series of reference patterns or chronologies, the date of each ring of which is known. When the growth-ring sequence of a sample "cross-matches" repeatedly at the same date span against a series of different relevant reference chronologies the sample can be said to be dated. The degree of cross-matching, that is the measure of similarity between sample and reference, is denoted by a "t-value"; the higher the value the greater the similarity. The greater the similarity the greater is the probability that the patterns of samples and references have been produced by growing under the same conditions at the same time. The statistically accepted fully reliable minimum t-value is 3.5.

However, rather than attempt to date each sample individually it

DENDROCHRONOLOGY REPORT

is usual to first compare all the samples from a single building, or phase of a building, with one another, and attempt to crossmatch each one with all the others from the same phase or building. When samples from the same phase do cross-match with each other they are combined at their matching positions to form what is known as a "site chronology". As with any set of data, this has the effect of reducing the anomalies of any one individual (brought about in the case of tree-rings by some non-climatic influence) and enhances the overall climatic signal. As stated above, it is the climate that gives the growth pattern its distinctive pattern. The greater the number of samples in a site chronology the greater is the climatic signal of the group and the weaker is the non-climatic input of any one individual.

Furthermore, combining samples in this way to make a site chronology usually has the effect of increasing the time-span that is under comparison. As also mentioned above, the longer the period of growth under consideration, the greater the certainty of the cross-match. Any site chronology with less than about 55 rings is generally too short for reliable dating.

Having obtained a date for the site chronology as a whole, the date spans of the constituent individual samples can then be found, and from this the felling date of the trees represented may be calculated. Where a sample retains complete sapwood, that is, it has the last or outermost ring produced by the tree before it was cut, the last measured ring date is the felling date of the tree. In the Tables and bar diagrams of this report, the retention of complete sapwood on a sample is denoted by upper case "C".

Sometimes, complete sapwood is found on a timber, but, because of its soft condition, some, or all of it, crumbles as the sample is cored. It is possible to measure how much of the sapwood part of the core has been lost and from this it is sometimes possible to estimate the number of rings the lost portion might have represented, From this it is possible to make a reasonable estimate the felling date of the timber. Such a state is represented by lower case "c" in the Tables and bar diagrams.

Where the sapwood is not complete it is necessary to calculate a likely felling date range for the tree. Such an estimate can be made with a high degree of reliability because oak trees generally have between 15 to 40 sapwood rings. For example, if a sample with, say, 12 sapwood rings has a last sapwood ring date of 1400, it is 95% probable that the tree represented was felled sometime between

1403 (1400+3 sapwood rings (12+3=15)) and 1428 (1400+28 sapwood rings (12+28=40)).

Given that in a timber-framed building the trees required for each phase are almost certainly to have been cut in a single felling operation especially for that building, it is usual to calculate the average date of the heartwood/sapwood boundary from all the dated samples from each phase of a building and add 15 to 40 rings to this average to get the likely overall felling date of all the timbers used. In this calculation, wide variations in the position/date of the heartwood/sapwood boundary (possibly suggesting different felling dates) must be noted and taken into consideration.

Analysis

In the case of the 10 samples obtained from 43 Hey Lane, each was prepared by sanding and polishing, and their annual growth-ring widths were measured. The data of these measurements were then compared with each other. At a minimum value of t=3.5 a single group comprising seven samples could be formed, cross-matching with each other at the positions indicated in the bar diagram, Figure 7. The seven cross-matching samples were combined at these indicated off-set positions to form a site chronology, HUDBSQ01, this having an overall length of 188 rings. Site chronology HUDBSQ01 was then satisfactorily dated by repeated and consistent comparison with a number of relevant reference chronologies for oak as spanning the years 1386 to 1573. The evidence for this dating is given in the t-values of Table 2.

Site chronology HUDBSQ01 was then compared with the three remaining measured samples but there was no further satisfactory cross-matching. Each of the three remaining samples was then compared individually with the full range of reference chronologies but there was, again, no further cross-matching and they must, therefore, remain undated.

Interpretation

Analysis by dendrochronology of 10 samples from this site has produced a single dated site chronology, HUDBSQ01, comprising seven samples, its 188 rings dated as spanning the years 1386 to 1573. However, although the seven samples overlap with each other to a certain extent, and cross-match with each other to produce a single site chronology, it would appear that at least two, and possibly three, phases of felling are represented.

As may be seen from the bar diagram, Figure 6, there is a considerable difference in the relative positions, and absolute dates, of the heartwood/sapwood boundary on some of the samples, and that, in effect, we appear to have two distinct sapwood periods. It will be seen from the bar diagram that one sub-group of samples, HUD-B02, B03, B05, and B07, have sapwood at a much earlier position and date than do samples HUD-B01, B08, and B09.

Indeed, one of the earlier samples, HUD-B03, retains complete sapwood, that is, it has the last ring produced by the tree it represents before it was felled. This last measured complete sapwood ring, and thus the felling of the tree, is dated to 1481. The relative position and date of the heartwood/sapwood boundary on the other three samples in this sub-group is such that they represent trees that were probably felled in 1481 as well.

The sapwood of the remaining three dated samples, HUD-B01, B08 and B09 is much later, though the actual felling date of the trees represented by these is a little less precise. One sample, HUDB09, is from a timber, the south-west purlin of the roof, which retains complete sapwood. However, a small portion of the sapwood, about 5mm, was lost during coring. It is estimated that this loss represent no more than 5-7 rings, and thus, given that the last extant sapwood ring on sample HUD-B09 is dated to 1573, it is estimated that the timber was felled, in round terms, approximately 1580.

It is possible that the timber represented by sample HUD-B01 (a wall plate), was also felled c.1580. However, given that the heartwood/sapwood boundary on this sample is dated to 1525, in order for this to have been the case the tree would have had 55 sapwood rings. Whilst this number of sapwood rings is not unheard of, it is above the 95% probability limit. Whilst this does not preclude it having been felled c.1580, the possibility that it was felled in the period 1540 to 1565 (i.e. 1525+15 to 1525+40), must also be considered.

Given that the third sample of this later group, HUD-B08, does not have a heartwood/sapwood boundary, it is not possible to give a felling date range for the timber represented. It is unlikely, however, given that its last measured heartwood ring is dated to 1532, to have been felled before 1547 (1532+15 - assuming the next ring the timber might have had was at the heartwood/sapwood boundary). It is therefore possible that the timber represented was felled at the same time as the timbers represented by either HUD-B01 or B09, but also possible that it was felled at another time altogether.

Conclusion

Given the evidence of the tree-ring dating it is clear that a number of timbers were felled in 1481. This probably represents the remains of the phase 1 timber-framed house of unknown date identified by the structural interpretation. Tree-ring dating also indicates the probable felling of further trees c.1580, these timbers probably representing the phase 2, late-sixteenth century, total rebuild also identified by the structural survey, and being the building seen on William Senior's map of 1634 as "William Peny – his Hey". It is in the final phase identified, phase 3, stylistically dated to c. 1780, that these older timbers are reused in conjunction with newly imported pine timbers.

The late-fifteenth and late-sixteenth century building phases represented by the dated timbers cannot be directly related to the documentary evidence. It would appear that the rent had increased from 2s 2d to 5s 1d by 1425, some 55 years before the 1481 house was built, and remained at this level in 1584, shortly after the house was supposedly re-worked. It is of course possible that the 1481 house detected here was not the first house on the site, but a replacement of one built after 1340, the building of which might account for the increase in rent. No evidence of such a house has been detected by this analysis. Why the rent did not increase by 1584 is unknown.

Three samples, HUD-B04, B06 and B10, remain ungrouped and undated. It will be seen from Table 1 that only sample HUD-B04, has sufficient rings, 70, for reliable analysis. There appears to be no particular problem with this sample such as complacent rings (showing little annual variation) or compressed or distorted rings, which might account for its remaining undated. This is a common feature of dendrochronology. The other two samples, HUD-B06 and B10, have marginal numbers of rings and while it is sometimes possible to date such cores, it is often more difficult where, as in this case, timbers of different dates are to be found, rather than in situations where large numbers of well-replicated, single-date, timbers are obtained.

Bibliography

Arnold, A J, Howard, R E, and Litton, C D, 2003 Tree-ring analysis of timbers from the Bell Frame and Tower Roof of St Margaret's Church, Wetton, Staffordshire, Centre for Archaeol Rep, 22/2003

Arnold, A J and Howard R E, Tree-ring analysis of timbers from All Hallow's Church, Kirkburton, West Yorkshire, Res Dep Rep Ser, 49/2007

Baillie, M G L, and Pilcher, J R, 1982 unpubl A master tree-ring chronology for England, unpubl computer file MGB-EOI, Queens Univ, Belfast

Fletcher, J, 1978 unpubl computer file MC10---H

Howard, R E, Laxton, R R, and Litton, C D, Nottingham University Tree-ring Dating Laboratory, and Roberts, H M, North East Vernacular Architecture Group, 1995 List 62 no 3a - Nottingham University Tree-Ring Dating Laboratory: buildings of the religious estates in medieval Durham; dendrochronological survey 1994 - 5, Vernacular Architect, 26, 55 – 6

Laxton, R R, and Litton, C D, 1988 An East Midlands master tree-ring chronology and its use for dating vernacular buildings, University of Nottingham, Dept of Classical and Archaeol Studies, Monograph Series, III

Morgan, R A, 1977 Dendrochronological dating of a Yorkshire Timber-framed building, Vernacular Architect, 8, 9 – 14

Tyers, I, 1997 Tree-ring Analysis of Timbers from Sinai Park, Staffordshire, Anc Mon Lab Rep, 80/1997

Table 1: Details of samples from "Peny's Hey", 43 Hey Lane, Lowerhouses, Huddersfield, West Yorkshire

Sample number	Sample location	Total rings	*Sapwood rings	First measured ring date	Last heartwood ring date	Last measured ring date
HUD-B01	Wall plate at rear window of living room	105	7	1428	1525	1532
HUD-B02	Ceiling beam in living room	57	13	1420	1463	1476
HUD-B03	Vertical post in living room	96	19C	1386	1462	1481
HUD-B04	Rear (south) wall plate to dining room	70	7	------	------	------
HUD-B05	Kitchen ceiling beam	62	9	1414	1466	1475
HUD-B06	Vertical post in dining room	53	13	------	------	------
HUD-B07	Bressummer to dining room fireplace	72	18	1408	1461	1479
HUD-B08	North-east purlin	82	no h/s	1425	------	1506
HUD-B09	South-west purlin	119	23c	1455	1550	1573
HUD-B10	North-west purlin	50	no h/s	------	------	------

*h/s = heartwood/sapwood boundary
c = complete sapwood is found on the timber, all or part has been lost from the sample during coring
C = complete sapwood retained on the sample, the last measured ring date is the felling date of the timber

Table 2: Results of the cross-matching of site chronology HUDBSQ01 and relevant reference chronologies when first ring date is 1386 and last ring date is 1573

Reference chronology	t-value	
England Master Chronology	8.4	(Baillie and Pilcher 1982 unpubl)
St Margaret's Church, Wetton, Staffs	7.7	(Arnold et al 2003)
Sinai Park, Burton on Trent, Staffs	7.6	(Tyers 1997)
SFF-B01M	7.5	(Morgan 1977)
All Hallow's Church, Kirkburton, W Yorks	7.4	(Arnold and Howard 2007)
Old Durham Farm, Durham	7.3	(Howard et al 1995)
MC10---H	7.0	(Fletcher 1978)
East Midlands Master Chronology	7.0	(Laxton and Litton 1988)

Figure 1: William Senior's Map of 1634 showing "William Peny – his Hey"

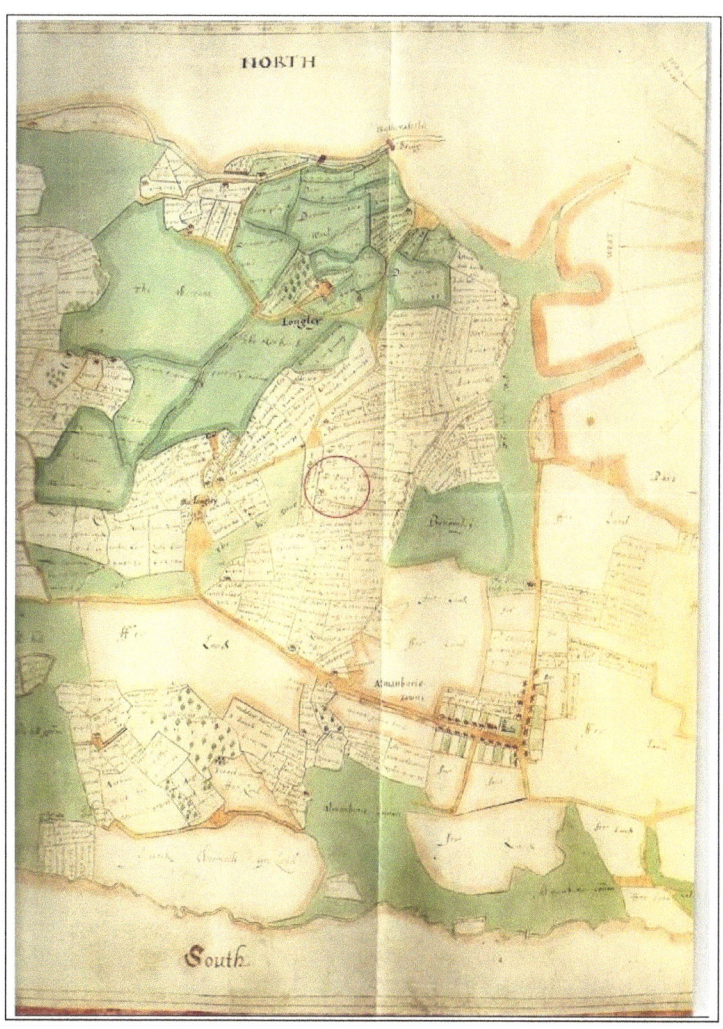

A HISTORY OF "PENY'S HEY"

Detail 1 from Figure 1:

DENDROCHRONOLOGY REPORT

Detail 2 from Figure 1:

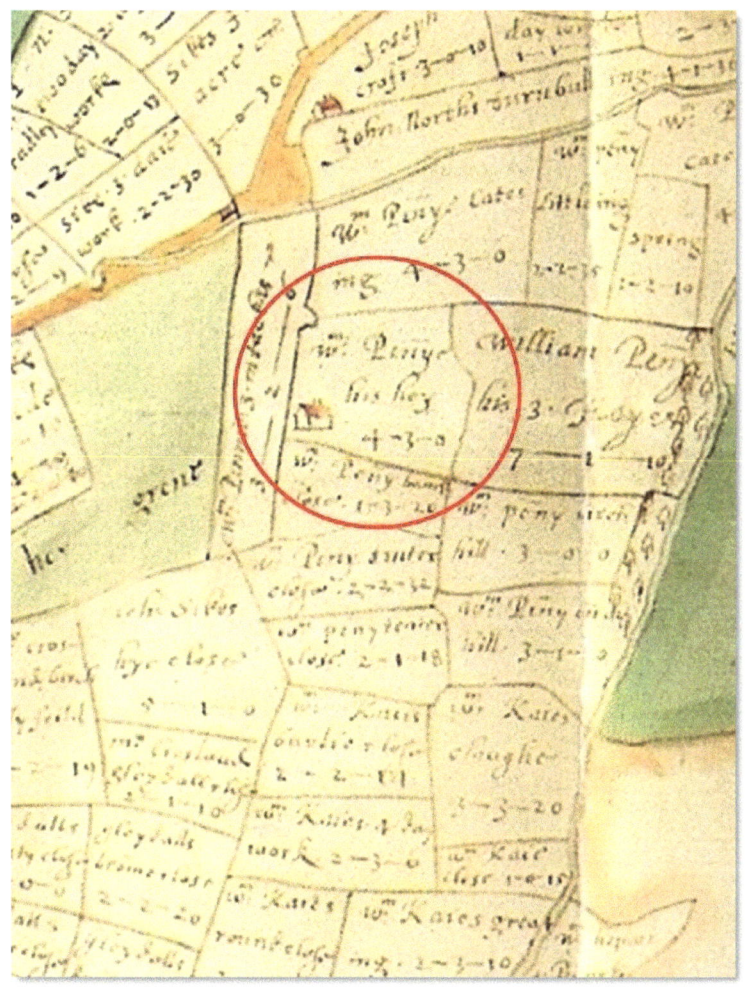

Figure 2: View of Peny's Hey prior to renovation

Figures 3a–c: Views of ground-floor timbers

Figure 3a: View of the ceiling beam and vertical post in the living room

Figure 3b: View of the ceiling beam in the kitchen

Figure 3c: View of the vertical post in the dining room

Figures 4a–b: Views of first-floor timbers

Figure 4a: View of the principal rafter truss

Figure 4b: View of the south-west purlin

Figures 5a–b: Simple sketch plans to show sample locations (not to scale)

Figure 5a: Ground floor

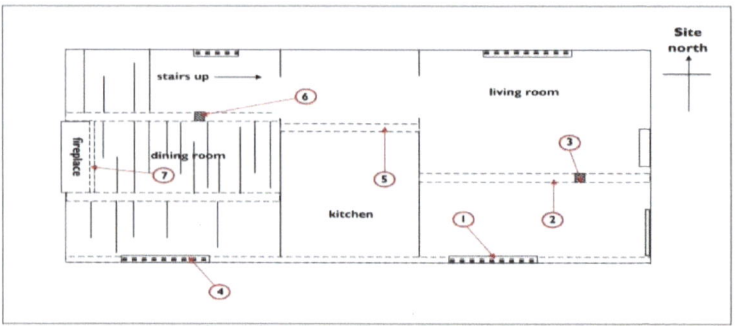

Figure 5b: First floor

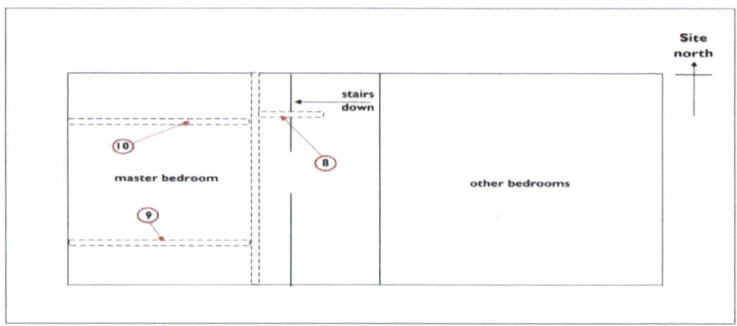

DENDROCHRONOLOGY REPORT

Figure 6: Bar diagram of the samples in site chronology HUDASQ01, sorted by likely felling phase

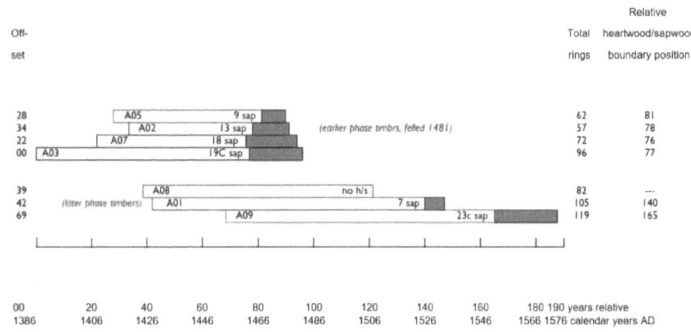

White bars = heartwood rings,
shaded area = sapwood rings
h/s = the last ring on the sample is at the heartwood/sapwood boundary; only the sapwood rings are missing
c = complete sapwood is found on the timber, all or part has been lost from the sample during coring
C = complete sapwood is retained on the sample, the last measured ring date is the felling date of the timber

www.ingramcontent.com/pod-product-compliance
Lightning Source LLC
LaVergne TN
LVHW010027070426
835510LV00001B/9